SEVEN STEPS TOWARD GOD

Seven Steps Toward God

BILL BEATTY
Foreword by Dorothy Ranaghan

GREENLAWN PRESS
South Bend, Indiana

First printing, January, 1986
Library of Congress Catalog Card Number: 85-082315
© 1986 by Greenlawn Press. All rights reserved.
Printed in the United States of America.

To Laurette

Bill Beatty is Executive Director for the National Service Committee of the Catholic Charismatic Renewal and a leader in the People of Praise, an ecumenical Christian community.

He graduated from St. Vincent College in 1959 and the Management Development Program at Harvard Business School in 1967. He left an executive career to teach at Aquinas High School in Augusta, Georgia, where he served as chairman of the Religion Department.

He has done extensive lay missionary work in the Caribbean and Latin America, and has spoken at many religious conferences throughout North America.

He is a native of New York City. His wife, Laurette, is a teacher and Dean of Girls at Trinity School at Greenlawn. The Beattys have three children and live in South Bend, Indiana.

Contents

Foreword 9

Introduction 11

Step One 16
   Accept God's Love

Step Two 28
   Accept God's Plan

Step Three 40
   Admit Your Needs

Step Four 50
   Decide to Change

Step Five....................... 62
   Give and Accept Forgiveness

Step Six 74
   Order Your Life

Step Seven 86
   Learn to Pray

Walking On 98

Foreword

"Keep it simple." This was my mother's approach to life. Whether it came to decorating a house (she hated bric-a-brac, which she called "dust-catchers") or to cooking food (preferring meat and potatoes to trendy fare), mom liked sticking to the essentials. She would like this book.

In *Seven Steps Toward God*, Bill Beatty has outlined the foundation stones upon which to build and maintain a sturdy love relationship with God. It is a no-frills book. Simply put, we need to know God's love for us and his plan for our lives, then accept ourselves, decide to change, ask and give forgiveness, put our lives in order, and learn to pray because prayer is the language of this love in which—rather, in whom—we live.

Living out the Christian life is not always simple or easy. In fact, it is often quite complex. Yet, the inexhaustible mystery of life in Christ is ultimately reducible to the stark reality of the cross—"for God so loved the world."

If you plan to treat yourself to a few hours or a few days alone with God, it might be a good idea to take this book with you. Each chapter concludes with a series of questions answered by a short text from the word of God, after which we are encouraged to give a written response, as the Spirit leads.

The wit and warmth and wisdom Bill brings to this subject give us new hope for what is possible in our task of growing in the love of God. After reading this book, I realize that it may be an uphill climb, but, like the little train in the storybook of my childhood, I found myself believing that one day I could stop saying merely, "I think I can, I think I can," but, rather, "I knew I could."

Dorothy Ranaghan

Introduction

We are all born with a longing in our hearts. This is the way God made us—with a deep-down longing, a hunger that wells up and cries out to be filled at the most surprising times. This longing may be the reason you bought or borrowed this little book. Something deep down inside you has moved you to seek more of God.

St. Augustine said, "You have made us for yourself, O Lord, and our hearts are restless until they rest in you." God has put this hunger in your heart. You may have tried to fill it with many things, some good, some bad, but nothing can fully quiet this restlessness or fill this void except God himself. God, who is all-just, is eager to fill it. If he put that hunger in you, he certainly will satisfy it.

Your life here on earth is a journey, with a lot of forks in the road. One leads to heaven; many lead to hell. Those going to hell lead you farther and farther away from God and other people. They bring you to greater and greater loneliness, isolation and fragmentation. These roads never lead anywhere. Your heart gets emptier as you go.

The road to heaven, on the other hand, leads deeper and deeper into the kingdom of God. It is narrow and difficult at times but you are traveling it with the Lord and with others who can help you on the way. As you go, you become more loving, peaceful and joyful. Your heart is filled as you travel the way of the Lord.

This book is about some first steps on the road leading to God. Proverbs says that this "path of the virtuous is like the light of dawn, its brightness growing to the fullness of day" (Pr. 4:18 JB). It is a path that ends when you see the Lord's face "shining brighter than the sun."

God is calling you now to hear and respond to his call to walk toward the "fullness of day," to experience his salvation in a new and deeper way, and to be strengthened, encouraged and better equipped for the journey.

There are no shortcuts on the road to heaven; no super-saver, cut-rate or bargain-basement fares. The road map is the same one that Jesus gave to the lawyer in Matthew 22: "You must love the Lord your God with all your heart, with all your soul, and with all your mind," and "you must love your fellow man as yourself" (TEV).

There are two stages to the journey. These are the two commands that God gives to all who start on the road to heaven: first, be reconciled to God. "Let God change you from enemies into friends! Christ was without sin, but for our sake God made him share our sin in order that we, in union with him, might share the righteousness of God" (II Cor. 5:20-21 TEV). Second, "you must put on the new self, which is created in God's likeness, and reveals itself in the true life that is upright and holy" (Eph. 4:24 TEV).

As you walk toward God you are called to an ongoing *metanoia*, an ongoing conversion of mind and heart. You are called to a normal Christian life, a life of holiness.

If this journey sounds very difficult or perhaps impossible, it is—if you try to make it by your own power. God, however, "is able to do so much more than we can ever ask for, or even think of, by means of his power working in us: to God be the glory in the church and in Christ Jesus, for all time, forever and ever! Amen" (Gal. 3:20-21 TEV).

You can read this little book in an evening. I'd prefer that you take it on your journey. Spend a week on each chapter. Take 15 minutes each day to reread the week's chapter and reflect on one of the daily meditations. Repeat the daily Scripture passage often throughout the day, and at the end of each week write down the response you want to give to the Lord.

I hope we meet along the way!

STEP ONE
ACCEPT GOD'S LOVE

"As the Father has loved me,
so have I loved you;
abide in my love."
John 15:9 (RSV)

STEP ONE: ACCEPT GOD'S LOVE

A world-famous theologian once gave a lecture to a learned university audience. As he finished, a young student in the crowd asked a question that embarrassed many of those present. He said, "Professor, in all your years of pastoral work and study you have learned so much. Could you tell me the most important thing you have learned?" The professor paused, then thoughtfully said, "Yet I can, son. 'Jesus loves me, this I know, for the Bible tells me so.'" He was applauded.

If you read the Bible, you must conclude that Jesus was either a madman, a fool, a liar or the Son of God he claimed to be. If you believe that he is the Son of God and that his words are true, then four facts should leap off the pages at you:

1. *God is love*!
2. *God* loves me!
3. God *loves* me!
4. God loves *me*!

Reading about these realities is easy, but it can be very difficult to get them from your head to your heart. It can be very difficult to accept fully the fact of God's love for you.

Yet, what underlies real healing—real progress in the Christian life—is the deep realization that God does love you, that he loves you perfectly, that he couldn't love you more even if he tried, that even before you were a Christian he loved you, that he chose to love you for no reason outside of himself, that he chose to love you because he wanted to, that you can't make him stop loving you, and that he chose to love you and to die for you while you were still his enemy.

The scandalous fact is this: Jesus crucified by your sins is the proof of God's love for you. You need to experience, believe and accept this realization.

Imagine that right now someone enters the very place where you are reading this and tells you that Jesus has appeared nearby and is asking him to bring you to him. Jesus wants to talk with you alone, now. You might experience some mixed emotions—excitement, joy and perhaps feelings of sinfulness, unworthiness and guilt.

Then turn and go out to meet the Lord.

19/STEP ONE: ACCEPT GOD'S LOVE

His face is radiant with love. Having put you at ease, he asks you a question, "Will you accept my love? Will you let me love you as I want to?"

Imagine what your honest response would be.

Why is it that you sometimes have such difficulty believing and accepting the fact of God's personal, constant, faithful love for you?

You know from God's word that he is for you, that he loves you perfectly and personally, that his love is constant, and that nothing can separate you from his love. Even so, one or more things can cripple your ability to accept that love.

The devil may be lying to you. The "accuser of the brethren" may be telling you that you are not really lovable, or he may be saying that God is angry or annoyed with you and doesn't really love you or that, if others knew you as you really are inside, they wouldn't love you, either.

You may also be crippled by the experience of a personal rejection. You may not have experienced the kind of human love that enables you to love yourself, to accept God's love, to love others.

Pehaps you may be living with a lingering awareness that your friendship with God has been damaged. You may need to repair that friendship and accept God's forgiveness.

You can believe with real certainty in God's boundless, personal, faithful love and forgiveness for others, but sometimes you can't believe with the same certainty in God's love for you, and because you can't you are unable to accept God's love fully.

How can you come to believe that God really loves you? How can you more fully accept that love?

First, if the devil has lied to you or if you have been crippled by human rejection, you need to make a decision to believe God's word to you in Ephesians 1:3-9 (RSV).

> Blessed be the God and Father of our Lord Jesus Christ, who has blessed us in Christ with every spiritual blessing in the

heavenly places, even as he chose us in him before the foundation of the world, that we should be holy and blameless before him. He destined us in love to be his sons through Jesus Christ, according to the purpose of his will, to the praise of his glorious grace which he freely bestowed on us in the Beloved. In him we have redemption through his blood, the forgiveness of our trespasses, according to the riches of his grace which he lavished upon us.

You may be crippled in your ability to accept God's love because you fail to remember God's love is pure gift. You don't deserve it. You can't earn it. It is God's free choice, and all you can do is accept it.

Second, if you struggle with feelings of sinfulness, unworthiness or guilt, which cripple your ability to be assured of God's love for you, you may need to repair your friendship with God. Then if you have done that and these feelings still linger you need to believe and accept God's word to you in Hebrews 10:15-22 (RSV):

And the Holy Spirit also bears witness to us; for after saying,

> "This is the covenant that I will make with them
> after those days, says the Lord:
> I will put my laws on their minds,"

then he adds,

> "I will remember their sins and their misdeeds no more."

Where there is forgiveness of these, there is no longer any offering for sin. Therefore, brethren, since we have confidence to enter the sanctuary by the blood of Jesus, by the new and living way which he opened for us through the curtain, that is, through his flesh, and since we have a great priest over the house of God, let us draw near with a true heart in full assurance of faith, with our hearts sprinkled clean from an evil conscience and our bodies washed with pure water.

Make a decision right now to believe that God loves you. No matter how you

STEP ONE: ACCEPT GOD'S LOVE

feel about it—God does love you, perfectly. Believe Jesus, the Word of God. Don't let the devil, or others, or circumstances, or past sins, or your misunderstandings hold you back from accepting what has already been given to you.

PRAYER: Lord Jesus, I can't earn it, I don't deserve it, but I accept your choice to love me. I believe that you are the Christ, the Son of the Living God. I believe that your word is true. Lord, I believe that you love me. Lord, I accept your love.

DAILY MEDITATION

1. *How do I know that God loves me?*

"God shows his love for us in that while we were yet sinners Christ died for us" (Rm. 5:8 RSV).

2. *What does God think of me right now?*

"You are precious in my eyes and honored, and I love you" (Is. 43:4 RSV)

3. *Does God's love for me change?*

"I have loved you with an everlasting love; therefore I have continued my faithfulness to you" (Jer. 31:3 RSV).

4. *Will God's love ever stop reaching me?*

"For I am sure that neither death nor life, nor angels, nor principalities, nor things present, nor things to come, nor powers, nor height, nor depth, nor anything else in all creation, will be able to separate us from the love of God in Christ Jesus our Lord" (Rm. 8:38-39 RSV).

25/STEP ONE: ACCEPT GOD'S LOVE

5. *Is God's love for me personal?*

"And I will be a father to you and you shall be my sons and daughters, says the Lord Almighty" (II Cor. 6:18 RSV).

6. *How do I know that God loves me personally?*

"When we cry Abba! Father! it is the Spirit himself bearing witness with our spirit that we are children of God" (Rm. 8:15-16 RSV).

7. *What is God's love really like?*

"The Lord is merciful and gracious, slow to anger and abounding in steadfast love" (Ps. 103:8 RSV).

My Response: _____

STEP TWO
ACCEPT GOD'S PLAN

"For I know the plans I have
for you, says the Lord, plans
for welfare and not for evil,
to give you a future
and a hope."
Jeremiah 29:11 (RSV)

STEP TWO: ACCEPT GOD'S PLAN

Scripture tells us that God has revealed his plan for mankind. "That secret is Christ himself; in him lie hidden all God's treasures of wisdom and knowledge" (Col. 2:2-3 NEB). In order to begin to appreciate the plan God has revealed to us in Jesus you need to understand the problem which his plan has saved you from.

The human race is in rebellion against God and against his plan. This rebellion is called sin. Because of the sin of mankind's first parents and the sin of mankind throughout history, the human race lives a cursed existence. Human beings could not reach God through their own efforts.

God's plan for saving mankind had to include pardon for the enormous sins committed throughout human history. It had to include reparation for the evil done. The hold of Satan and his followers had to be broken. Justice had to be established. The curses of disease and death had to be overcome. Men and women had to experience a change in their very nature so that they would be able to live in a way that would please God.

It is obvious that the solution was beyond the ability or power of mankind. The solution could only come from the one that mankind had rebelled against, God himself.

Jesus is the perfect fulfillment of God's plan. By his birth, death and resurrection he has won the victory for us. Sin is forgiven, reparation is made, Satan is defeated, justice is established, disease and death defeated, and individuals can be born again by the power of God's Holy Spirit.

God's plan is that each human being submit to Jesus, come under his Lordship, receive the gift of his Holy Spirit, become part of his body and be led by him to the Father. God's plan for the human race provides a first installment, a pledge, a foretaste of what is to come when Jesus comes again. When men and women accept God's plan, they can begin to experience God's salvation in the smallest events of their daily lives, making them sons and daughters, saving them from their enemies, delivering them from the work of evil spirits, healing them and giving them abundant new life.

God is a living God. He lives in individuals in the power of his Spirit and he has a plan for his saving action in each person's life that he wants to reveal so each person can accept it.

God's call to you today is recorded in Matthew 22: "You must love the Lord your God with all your heart, with all your soul, and with all your mind," and "you must love your fellow-man as yourself" (TEV). The Jews called this the "great shema," the "yoke of heaven."

Jesus told us his yoke is "light" and "good to bear." The power of the Holy Spirit makes it so, and Jesus promised that, if anyone believed in him and came to him, rivers of this power would flow from his heart.

This is the same power which raised Jesus from the dead. It is all the power you need to live a holy life. So you don't have to be fearful or anxious about embracing the fullness of God's plan for your life.

Growth in holiness is God's plan for you, but it is a process never completed until you see the Lord face to face. "The path of the virtuous is like the light of dawn, its brightness growing to the fullness of day" (Pr. 4:18 JB). God calls you to press on in accepting the fullness of his plan for you.

The Lord tells you, "I will instruct you and teach you the way you should go; I will counsel you with my eye upon you" (Ps. 32:8 RSV). *God's plan is that you love him with your whole heart, mind and strength, and, in loving him this way, be led by him.*

You can struggle for years trying to discern the daily details of God's plan for your life because you reverse the sequence. You put the emphasis on discovering what God's plans are rather than on seeking to live in deep union with him.

The orientation you should have is seeking the Lord first and choosing him in every situation, including the smallest events of your daily lives. Discerning God's plan should be part of a way of life,

STEP TWO: ACCEPT GOD'S PLAN

not an occasional activity you attempt when you are faced with the need to make a major decision. Of course, you can really desire to discover God's plan for your life and to do it, yet still continue to stumble and grope for direction, confused by your fears and doubts, because you lack discernment.

Nevertheless, discerning God's plan for yourself does not have to elude your grasp or remain an occasional activity focussed on the extraordinary, the pounding heart, the goosebumps, the fleece or the prophetic word. Discernment can be amazingly practical and rooted in your ordinary, everyday, human experiences which have been made extraordinary by Jesus who became a human being.

God's wisdom is available to you to help you discover God's plan for the smallest details of your life. He can fill your daily life with the power and love and direction of the Holy Spirit. The key to discerning God's plan for you is living in deep union with him.

Here are some practical steps you can

take to grow in union with God and in your ability to be led by him:

1) Offer your life to the Lord daily. Make it the goal of your daily life to love God with your whole heart, mind and strength.

2) Pray daily for an increase of faith and trust in the Lord's plan for your life.

3) Reflect prayerfully each day on your experiences. Discover God's plan working out in the smallest events of your daily life.

4) Discuss your discernment with mature Christians, and open your life to the light of Christ with either a regular confessor, spiritual director or pastoral advisor.

It will become easier to discover God's plan for your life in times of major crisis or decision if you have acquired the ability to hear the still, small voice of the Holy Spirit at all times. Then, in a heartfelt attitude of ready obedience you can accept the Lord's plan and you can say, "all that the Lord has spoken, [I] will do" (Ex. 19:8 RSV).

STEP TWO: ACCEPT GOD'S PLAN

PRAYER: Lord Jesus, I thank you for being the perfect fulfillment of the Father's plan of salvation. I thank you for the salvation that you have won for me. Baptize me in your Holy Spirit anew each day and let me live in deep union with you and come to know and accept your plan for my life.

DAILY MEDITATION

1. *Why should I accept God's plan?*

"I am the way, and the truth and the life; no one comes to the Father but by me" (Jn. 14:6 RSV).

2. *What is the secret of God's plan?*

"That secret is Christ himself; in him lie hidden all God's treasures of wisdom and knowledge" (Col. 2:2,3 NEB).

3. *Why am I afraid of God's plan for me?*

"There is no fear in love, but perfect love casts out fear. For fear has to do with punishment, and he who fears is not perfected in love" (1 Jn. 4:18 RSV).

4. *How can I find God's plan each day?*

"Thy word is a lamp to my feet and a light to my path" (Ps. 119:105 RSV).

5. *Will I miss a lot of fun if I fully accept God's plan?*

STEP TWO: ACCEPT GOD'S PLAN

"But Jesus answered: 'Rather, how happy are those who hear the word of God and obey it' " (Lk. 11:28 RSV).

6. *Will God make his plans known to me?*

"And your ears shall hear a word behind you saying, this is the way, walk in it, when you turn to the right or when you turn to the left" (Is. 30:21 RSV).

7. *Does God keep changing his plans for me?*

"God wanted to make it very clear to those who were to receive what he promised that he would never change his purpose; so he added his vow to the promise" (Heb. 6:17 TEV).

My Response:

STEP THREE
ADMIT YOUR NEEDS

"And my God will supply
every need of yours
according to his riches
in glory in Christ Jesus."
Philippians 4:19 (RSV)

STEP THREE: ADMIT YOUR NEEDS

God is the God of Exodus. He is always calling you "out of darkness and into his wonderful light." He is always calling you to admit your needs and to allow him to bring his saving light into the deepest and darkest corners of your heart. The Good News is that God wants to love you and save you even more than you are ready to accept.

This chapter could also be titled "Fake It or Make It." After all, you could accept God's love and surrender to his plans but still not make much progress in your spiritual journey because you fail to bring into the light many areas of your life in which you need to experience the saving action of God.

You may not be very good at admitting your needs. You can repress them, for instance, or try to hide them, or even convince yourself that they don't exist.

Many years ago I sat in church and heard a preacher give a sermon on "Jesus the Trash Man." My first reaction was to bristle at his choice of words, but his message was really helpful. The idea was that our sins are like trash. Jesus is willing to remove them, but we have to allow him to help us.

If you leave the kitchen door unlocked, the Lord will enter and take out the trash. Actually, he won't just remove the trash from the kitchen; he will renovate the kitchen.

If you open the door to the dining room, the closets, the attic, the basement, he will do the same. If you give to the Lord the key to each room in your heart, he will enter each room and make it new. If my mother had learned that the president of the United States was going to pay a surprise visit to her home in 15 minutes, I'm sure that a lot of things would quickly find their way into the nearest closet or drawer. I'm sure that when the president arrived she would not lead him directly to those closets and drawers and proudly display all the items she had hidden.

You might act the same way with the Lord. You might insist on trying to tidy up areas of your life by your own strength before you give him access, and thereby fail

43/STEP THREE: ADMIT YOUR NEEDS

to obtain the healing and forgiveness and restoration that he has for you.

There are many rooms in your heart that urgently need the saving action of God, many areas where you need to face up to reality and cry out to the Lord, "Jesus, save me!"

The Lord wants your life to be an oasis of his love, not a mirage. When you first meet the Lord, you open your life to him and honestly confess your sins and tell him of your deepest needs. Then, as time passes, you begin to pull back from that depth of openness. Time after time, you need to make a decision to admit your needs honestly and openly to the Lord so that you might experience his forgiveness and healing.

If you keep your problems in the dark they fester and grow. Jesus is the light of the world, and darkness cannot overcome it. "Anything exposed by the light will be illuminated and anything illuminated turns into light" (Eph. 5:13-14 JB).

The Apostle John states it even more clearly: "This is the message we have heard from him and proclaim to you, that God is light and in him is no darkness at all. If we say we have fellowship with him while we walk in darkness, we lie and do not live according to the truth; but if we walk in the light, as he is in the light, we have fellowship with one another, and the blood of Jesus his Son cleanses us from all sin" (1 Jn. 1:5-9 RSV).

Many people become committed Christians because they encounter a need in their lives that only God can meet. They have discovered in a very real way their need for a savior.

However, it is also possible for those same people to begin to accept Jesus as Lord and to become his disciples, but still not surrender a great many of the needs and problems in their lives. They might do this for several reasons. They could insist on meeting those needs from their own strength, or they could play all sorts of games with themselves and deny or repress the existence of the problem.

Jesus calls you to put your life fully under the scrutiny of his light and to admit

45/STEP THREE: ADMIT YOUR NEEDS

all your needs. He wants you to stop trying to be savior of your own life and to surrender everything to him, including your deepest needs.

Jesus is the good shepherd. He knows you. He knows you as you have been and as you are now. He loved you even in your worst moments. There is no way of hiding anything from him. The thing is, you don't have to. He loves you as you are. This can be frightening, of course—to know that someone knows everything about you, your worst thoughts, feelings, actions. Still, you must let God determine the way of salvation.

Salvation means accepting the personal knowing and loving of Jesus for you. Only in this acceptance of the love of the risen Christ are your aloneness and insecurity and inability to admit your needs fully conquered.

Jesus is the way. As you experience the presence and power and love of Jesus, you are freed and transformed. Hate becomes love, anxiety becomes peace, suspicion becomes trust, weakness becomes strength and your aloneness is filled by the presence of God.

Jesus is the truth. Face to face with him you know the truth about him, about yourself, about your needs, about the value of material things, about the value of the world, life and death.

Jesus is the life. You are never more truly alive than when you live in love. When the one who knows you totally also loves you totally, you not only have life but you have it abundantly.

The love of Jesus sets you free. "If the Son sets you free, you are free indeed" (Jn. 8:36 RSV). You are freed from fear, freed from insecurity, freed from self-centeredness, freed to admit your deepest needs to yourself, to the Lord and to others.

Prayer: Lord Jesus, I believe that you are the light that has come into the world. I believe that your light can drive out the darkness in my life. Lord, give me the strength to admit my needs and bring them out of the darkness and into your light.

STEP THREE: ADMIT YOUR NEEDS

DAILY MEDITATION

1. *Sometimes I'm dry and joyless. God seems distant.*

"You will seek me and find me; when you seek me with all your heart, I will be found by you, says the Lord" (Jer. 29:13 RSV).

2. *Sometimes I feel guilty and fear God's judgment.*

"If we confess our sins, he is faithful and just, and will forgive our sins and cleanse us from all unrighteousness" (1 Jn. 1:9 RSV).

3. *Sometimes I'm concerned about my health and finances.*

"The Lord is my shepherd, I shall not want" (Ps. 23:1 RSV).

4. *Sometimes I feel confused, powerless. I'm drifting.*

"And I will lead the blind in a way they know not, in paths they have not known I will guide them. I will turn the darkness before them into light, the rough places into level ground" (Is. 42:15 RSV).

5. *Sometimes I feel alone, overwhelmed by temptation.*

"Resist the devil and he will flee from you. Draw near to God and he will draw near to you" (Jm. 4:7-8 RSV).

6. *Sometimes I struggle with depression, loneliness, grief.*

"The Lord is near to the brokenhearted, and serves the crushed in spirit" (Ps. 35:18 RSV).

7. *Sometimes I'm fearful and anxious.*

"For God did not give us a spirit of timidity but a spirit of power and love and self-control" (II Tim. 1:7 RSV).

49/STEP THREE: ADMIT YOUR NEEDS

My Response: _____

_____

_____

_____

_____

_____

_____

STEP FOUR
DECIDE TO CHANGE

"Do not be conformed
to this world but be
transformed by the renewal
of your mind. . . ."
Romans 12:2 (RSV)

STEP FOUR: DECIDE TO CHANGE

From time to time I take a crumpled piece of paper from my wallet and read seven questions written there years ago:

1) Has serious sin been cleaned up in my life?
2) Is less serious sin diminishing?
3) Is the fruit of the Spirit more apparent in my life, and are the works of the flesh diminishing?
4) Am I more willing to admit my mistakes, repair wrongdoing and accept correction from others?
5) Am I using more of my time, talent and money for the Lord?
6) Am I faithful to a daily prayer time?
7) Does my life flow into loving service to the Lord and to others?

Some prayerful consideration of these seven questions always brings me to the same conclusion. I must decide to change. I must decide anew to "be reconciled to God" and "to put on the new self."

I realize once again that I am a sinner called to daily joyful repentance and utter dependence on the Lord's mercy, forgiveness and strength, but I also realize again that I must take responsibility for my actions and really decide to change. That's also where I find the struggle.

There are three things you struggle with when God confronts you with the need to take responsibility for your actions and to make a decision to change.

These three obstacles can block the transformation of our hearts: the devil, the world and the flesh.

The first thing you must do is to choose sides in a cosmic struggle. God calls you to become obedient servants, like Jesus. The devil will do all he can to frustrate this, but you have the power to rebuke the devil.

Second, you must come to terms with what St. John calls "the world" (I Jn. 2:16 RSV), that system of values which is hostile to Jesus and his kingdom. You should not reject the created order that God instituted and loves, but you must reject the worldly values which call us to "lord it over" others and "make our importance felt."

53/STEP FOUR: DECIDE TO CHANGE

Third, you must deal with those values, attitudes and behavior in yourself which are opposed and hostile to the gospel. Wounded by Adam's sin, you are constantly drawn to think about yourself and to choose ways that are self-serving. "The flesh in its tendency is at enmity with God; it is not subject to God's law" (Rm. 8:7 NAB).

St. Paul, however, tells us that "the Spirit helps us in our weakness, . . . and intercedes for the saints as God himself wills" (Rm. 8:26,27 NAB). Jesus calls you to wage war with the flesh and sends his Spirit to transform you into a loving servant motivated by love for him and for all mankind.

In all three cases the bottom line is that you must make a daily decision to die to yourself. It's a decision to change those things in your heart and in your actions that are not in conformity with God's plan.

I am reminded again that the seed must fall to the ground and die. In trying to hold on to my life I will lose it, but, if I lose it for the sake of the Lord, I will find it. The struggle is real because I am being asked to die, and it is often very hard to decide to change. Sometimes the most honest response I can give to the Lord is that I want to be more willing to change, and ask him to change my stony heart into a heart of flesh.

Some Christians have real difficulty when God calls them to make a decision to change because they view loving God as a means to something rather than as an end in itself. They subordinate the love of God to other goals and ideals in their lives (which might include personal comfort or material success). Christianity for them is just one of many activities and commitments in their lives.

Other Christians have difficulty deciding to change areas of their lives to conform with God's plan because they have no real priorities in their lives. They pursue conflicting goals, which then compete for first place: Christianity, financial security, success in business and so on.

The real solution to these problems is to make a decision. It is the best decision

55/STEP FOUR: DECIDE TO CHANGE

any Christian can make if he or she is serious about deciding to change and to live consistently in accord with God's plan. It is simply to decide to make loving God the ideal of one's whole life.

You are called to love God with your whole heart. In Scripture the heart is the place of fundamental choice. When you choose to make loving God with your whole heart the ideal of your life, you are making a truly fundamental choice.

It is fundamental because every other judgment, choice, decision you make will be based upon that prior choice. That decision will provide an orientation that will shape your entire life. It is a commitment to seek the Lord first, to place his will and interests above your own no matter what the cost.

If you want to accept God's love, to accept God's plan, to admit your needs and to decide to change and live in conformity with God's plan, then you have to be more than merely *interested* in loving God. Loving God needs to become the ideal of your life, the aim of your life, the direction in which everything in your life points.

If loving God with all your heart is not the ideal of your life and if you have real struggles making the right choices, then you need to make a conscious choice to make that decision.

There are three good reasons for making the decision:
1) God is worth it. God deserves it. Nothing compares with him.
2) You were created to love him. It is the purpose of life itself. If you ignore this, you will be frustrated and unhappy.
3) God commanded you to love him. Jesus didn't *suggest* that you love God, he *insisted* on it.

Loving God is not just something you feel. It is primarily something you *do*, especially when you decide to change and conform your mind to the mind of Christ.

If you make this conscious choice to take loving God as the principal aim of your life, then you will find a growing clarity in your Christian life and in your decisions. Every judgment, choice and de-

STEP FOUR: DECIDE TO CHANGE

cision you make will move you closer and closer to the mind of God, closer to putting on the mind of Christ, closer to being so changed that someday you might say with St. Paul, "It is no longer I who live, but Christ who lives in me" (Gal. 2:20 RSV).

Prayer: Lord Jesus, I want to make a decision to change my life. I want to make loving God with my whole mind, heart and strength the ideal of my whole life. Send your Spirit to guide and strengthen me, that I might always place your plans above my own.

DAILY MEDITATION

1. *Will God give me the desire and ability to change?*

"God is always at work in you to make you willing and able to obey his own purpose" (Ph. 2:13 TEV).

2. *Will God show me what I need to change?*

"I will instruct you and teach you the way you should go; I will counsel you with my eye upon you" (Ps. 32:8 RSV).

3. *I'm afraid to try to change some things.*

"Behold, I have given you authority to tread upon serpents and scorpions, and over all the power of the enemy; and nothing shall hurt you" (Lk. 10:19 RSV).

4. *I don't have the will-power to change some things.*

"I can do all things in him who strengthens me" (Ph. 4:13 RSV).

STEP FOUR: DECIDE TO CHANGE

5. *If I try and then fail, will God be angry?*

"Return to the Lord your God, for he is gracious and merciful, slow to anger, and abounding in streadfast love" (Jl. 3:13 RSV).

6. *Will God help me to keep my promises?*

"He gives power to the faint, and to him who has no might he increases strength" (Is. 40:29 RSV).

7. *If I try, will God change my heart?*

"I will take the stony heart out of their flesh and give them a heart of flesh that they may walk in my statutes and keep my commandments" (Ez. 11:19-20 RSV).

My Response: _____

STEP FIVE
ASK AND GIVE FORGIVENESS

"For if you forgive men their trespasses, your heavenly Father also will forgive you: but if you do not forgive men their trespasses, neither will your Father forgive your trespasses."
Matthew 6:14-15 (RSV)

STEP FIVE: ASK AND GIVE FORGIVENESS

The key to experiencing salvation is conversion from sin. This means daily repentance, asking forgiveness from God and from those you have injured, and being quick to forgive those who have injured you.

Unrepented sin and unforgiveness is like poison in the spiritual life. It begins to affect every part of you: body, mind and spirit. King David experienced the price of unrepented sin. In Psalm 32:3-5 (RSV) he wrote about it:

> When I declared not my sin, my body wasted away,
> through my groaning all day long.
> For day and night thy hand was heavy upon me;
> my strength was dried up as by the heat of summer.
> I acknowledged my sin to thee,
> and I did not hide my iniquity;
> I said, "I will confess my transgressions to the Lord";
> then thou didst forgive the guilt of my sin.

David refused for a time to take responsibility for his sin, and he paid a great price. One commentator said that God can't make you repent, but he can sure make you wish you had. When David admitted his sin and repented, he was reconciled to God and his guilt was lifted.

Any failure to deal with sin in your life, to admit responsibility and seek forgiveness will produce a deadly effect on your spiritual life, your relationships and sometimes on your physical and emotional health as well.

You may not be guilty of murder and adultery—David's situation is, after all, somewhat dramatic—but the principle is the same. Unrepented sin wreaks havoc in your life.

There are many passages in Scripture that call people to an initial turning away from sin, but there are also just as many passages addressed to committed Christians who have become lukewarm. In Revelation the Lord says, "Those whom I love I reprove and chasten, so be zealous and repent" (3:19 RSV). The Lord is calling us to ongoing repentance—daily repentance—as a way of life.

The Aramaic word which the Jews used for "repentance" means "to turn completely around." In the New Testament, the Greek word "*metanoia*" is used. It means to take a different course of action, to have a change of mind.

"Repentance" means turning from one direction to a new one. For the Christian, this means turning from sin and turning toward God. It is an action you take, a decision you make, and it does not depend on whether or not you feel guilt or sorrow. It is a decision which brings a change in your direction.

All human beings are sinners. Romans 3:23 (RSV) tells us, "All have sinned and fallen short of the glory of God." Because of the sin of our first parents, there is a resistance in us which pulls at us to break our relationship with God.

Two ways in which Scripture talks about sin are: one, as an offense against God, and two, as a power that holds us enslaved. When Moses chastized the Israelites for their sin, he told them they had broken their covenant with God. Sin itself is breaking our personal covenant with God.

St. Paul talks about the power of sin as something that holds you enslaved. As a force, sin entered the world through mankind's first parents and has continued to wreak havoc through the constant sin of mankind down through history. When John the Baptist referred to Jesus as "the Lamb of God who takes away the sin of the world" (Jn. 1:29 RSV) he was revealing the answer to the sinful condition that fills the world and enslaves human beings in this life.

Scripture is clear: sin is not a power from which you can escape by yourself. Salvation must come from God. You can't reach salvation on your own, but God has reached us in Jesus, the savior of the world.

The grace to repent is a gift from God. You can't earn it, you don't deserve it. You can only receive it in faith when God gives it to you. Reliant on the grace to repent, you can make the decision to repent.

STEP FIVE: ASK AND GIVE FORGIVENESS

When the Spirit of God convicts you of sin and gives you the grace of repentance, you need to admit your responsibility, repent and turn back to the Lord. You need to act on the gift of grace and not waste it.

It is amazing to see how many great saints speak of their sinfulness. The reason is that, the closer they came to God and the more the Holy Spirit was working in them, the more they were convicted of sin and saw their need for forgiveness. Early on, St. Paul referred to himself as "the last of the Apostles"; next he referred to himself as "the least of the Apostles," and toward the end of his ministry he referred to himself as "not worthy to be called an Apostle." St. Paul was not backsliding; he was coming closer to the light of Christ.

As you move toward God, the Holy Spirit will convict you of sin in several ways. First, he will convict you of intentional sin. When you have deliberately been unfaithful to God and you are convicted of that sin you need to acknowledge your guilt and repent immediately.

The Holy Spirit will also convict you of

the roots of sin in your life. When you see a pattern of sin that you have repented for repeatedly but continue to commit, the Spirit will reveal the root of that sin and convict you of it. You will be taught by God that pride, for example, is the root of unkind speech.

Another way that the Holy Spirit works in you is to show you areas of weakness in your life which may not involve sinful acts. They may be such things as failure to shoulder some of the responsibilities of your state in life. Even though these failures may not be sinful, you will have God's help in overcoming them.

These are four simple steps in asking forgiveness from God. First, you need to admit that you have broken apart the relationship. Second, you need to accept responsibility for your action. Third, you need to resolve not to do it again, and to make restitution. Fourth, you need to ask and accept God's forgiveness. These steps are the same when you need to ask the forgiveness of another person whom you have injured.

STEP FIVE: ASK AND GIVE FORGIVENESS

What about giving forgiveness? You must forgive if you are to be forgiven. Harboring unforgiveness is also poison in your life. If you want to make progress toward God you must forgive those who have injured you. You need to say to those who ask your forgiveness, "yes, I forgive you," not excuses such as "oh, it didn't bother me." Then you need to follow the Lord's example. He forgives and forgets.

You should forgive from the heart and show this forgiveness with concrete acts of renewed commitment and affection. Relating in this way can heal the damages of past injuries and strengthen you to serve the Lord and other people in peace and joy.

Asking and giving forgiveness should be a joyful occasion. There is great "joy in heaven over one sinner who repents" (Lk. 15:7 RSV) and you should share in that joy.

Prayer: Lord Jesus, I thank you that you are "the Lamb of God who takes away the sin of the world." Send your Spirit each day to convict me of the sin in my life and give me the grace of daily, joyful repentance. Lord, help me to forgive others as you forgive me.

STEP FIVE: ASK AND GIVE FORGIVENESS

DAILY MEDITATION

1. *If I ask forgiveness will God restore me?*

"If you repent, I will restore you that you may serve me" (Jn. 15:19 NIV).

2. *Can I rely on God's forgiveness?*

"If we confess our sins, he is faithful and just and will forgive us our sins and purify us from all unrighteousness" (1 Jn. 1:9 NIV).

3. *Why does God forgive me?*

"I am the God who forgives your sins, and I do this because of who I am" (Is. 43:25 GN).

4. *Will God hold my past sins against me?*

"I will forgive their iniquity and never call their sin to mind" (Jer. 31:34 JB).

5. *How should I forgive others?*

"Put on, then, as God's chosen ones, holy and beloved, compassion, kindness, lowliness, meekness and patience, forbearing one another and, if one has a complaint against another, forgiving each other; as the Lord has forgiven you, so also must you forgive. And above all these put on love which binds everything together in perfect harmony" (Col. 3:12-14 RSV).

6. *Can I get help if I find it very hard to forgive?*

Jesus "is able to do so much more than we can ever ask for, or even think of, by means of the power working in us" (Eph. 3:20 TEV).

7. *I am afraid of falling again.*

"No temptation has overtaken you that is not common to man. God is faithful, and he will not let you be tempted beyond your strength, but with the temptation will also provide the way of escape that you may be able to endure it" (1 Cor. 10:13 RSV).

73/STEP FIVE: ASK AND GIVE FORGIVENESS

My Response: _____

_____

_____

_____

_____

_____

_____

STEP SIX
ORDER YOUR LIFE

"If any of you lacks wisdom, let him ask God, who gives to all men generously and without reproaching, and it will be given him."
James 1:5 (RSV)

STEP SIX: ORDER YOUR LIFE

> Mary had a little lamb,
> It never became a sheep.
> It became a committed Christian
> and died from lack of sleep!
> (Unknown)

Many committed Christians become overcommitted—not to the Lord, but to a variety of other interests and activities. The result is insufficient sleep and exercise, irregular prayer time, strained relationships at home and at work. You can get away with this for a time, but inevitably the result is burnout and discouragement. It happens when you fail to put order in your life.

Yes, the Lord does want you to grow in generosity and to lay your life down in service to the church and to the world, but he also wants to give you his wisdom on how you should serve him.

Ninety percent of the solution is admitting that your life is not in order and believing that with prayerful common sense and God's power you can do something about it. You may be one of those who struggle with the fear that they really can't get their lives in good order and keep it that way. You need to fight this fear with God's truth, which tells you that you can change and "do all things in him who strengthens [you]" (Ph. 4:13 RSV).

Second, you need to expose your life to the light of Christ. You need to set aside time to pray for the grace to see your duties clearly as God sees them, and to see those obstacles and excuses which have kept you from following God's plan for your life. If defiance of authority, impulsiveness, laziness or procrastination cripples your life, you need to repent and pray for the desire and strength to change.

Once your heart is fixed on the Lord, if you find that you need to admit quite honestly that your life is not in order, if you sincerely want to change and if you believe by God's power you can change, then make two decisions:

1) Decide to put your life in order by establishing priorities and developing a personal schedule.

STEP SIX: ORDER YOUR LIFE

2) Make it a top priority and schedule the time necessary to buy, study and act on the excellent practical wisdom on ordering your personal schedule which is available on the shelves of most Christian bookstores.

St. Thomas said it well: "grace builds on nature." If we are serious about growth in the Christian life, we need to begin on ground level by ordering our priorities, ordering our time and making sure that we get proper sleep, exercise, diet and recreation.

Next, consider some basic decisions you may need to make in the four key areas of your Christian life: prayer, fellowship, study and service.

1) Prayer. If you want to move toward God you must become a person of prayer. There are five major forms of prayer, each of them essential in the Christian life: praise, repentance, thanksgiving, listening and intercession. Make a decision to schedule 30 minutes of personal prayer each day during which time you praise, repent, thank, listen and intercede. Make a

decision to fast at least part of one day each week, because the Lord considered prayer and fasting to be complementary efforts in our relationship with him.

2) Fellowship. Make it a top priority to find the place in the body of Christ where God wants you to be, the place in which you can be called to holiness, strengthened and equipped for service, corrected, taught, encouraged and built up "into the full stature of Christ."

3) Study. The study of Scripture is necessary if you are to understand fully what God is saying to you. Scripture study can be hard work, and it might be an area where you have to pick up your cross. Make a decision to read Scripture prayerfully 15 minutes per day, to study Scripture at least one hour per week and to read at least one good spiritual book each month.

4) Service. Ask yourself how you are using your time, talents and money in the service of the Lord. The two key possessions over which we have any control are our time and our money. Loving God

STEP SIX: ORDER YOUR LIFE

"with our whole strength" has a lot to do with how we spend our time and how we spend our money. Everything we have belongs to God, not just one-tenth. Decide to discover God's plan for you in this respect through prayer and advice from mature Christian friends.

Bringing order into the areas of prayer, fellowship, study and service must be accompanied by bringing order into two other key areas, family life and finances.

Several years ago I listened to a respected pastor tell this story. A man in his church came to him to discuss the call he felt to Christian leadership and his desire to be a shepherd. The man's wife was also present, and appeared quite upset and angry. The pastor noted that the couple related to each other in a harsh way. He asked the man, "Is this your first sheep?"

Here's a story from my own life. Many years ago I arrived at the location for a weekly prayer meeting which I was scheduled to lead. Three people from the group asked me to step aside for a conversation. When we were by ourselves, they asked me not to lead that meeting and not to lead any more meetings until they saw better fruit in my marriage and family life.

I left angry and upset, but I know that the Lord was speaking to me through them. I reflected on how my family was doing, and discovered that we were lacking the order needed to flourish. As a result, I dedicated myself to being a better husband and father. As the weeks passed my marriage and family life blossomed and I was eventually called back into service.

Those three brothers gave me some of the best advice I've ever been given, and I thank God that he blessed me with Christian friends who loved me enough to speak the truth and to call me to put my life in order.

The family is the basic cell in the body of Christ. A family that lives in deep Christian love and in unity of mind and heart really lifts Jesus up before the world and is one of the most effective forms of evangelism.

You should not be attempting significant

STEP SIX: ORDER YOUR LIFE

Christian service if your family life or finances are in disorder. If your finances are not in order make a decision to get competent help. Bringing the problem out into the light and seeking God's wisdom will take you a long way toward a proper solution. The Lord wants you to live within your means. He will provide for all your needs, not necessarily all your wants.

"God is not a God of confusion but of peace" (1 Cor. 14:33 RSV). He doesn't want you to be overwhelmed or to lack his peace as you attempt to order your life. His wisdom and strength are available to you.

Prayer: Lord Jesus, you are a God of order, not confusion. Send your Holy Spirit to help me make the choices necessary to put my life in order and strengthen me to carry out those decisions.

DAILY MEDITATION

1. *On prayer*

"But when you pray, go into your room and shut the door and pray to your Father in secret; and your Father who sees in secret will reward you" (Mt. 6:6 RSV).

2. *On family*

"But if anyone does not take care of his relatives, especially the members of his own family, he has denied the faith and is worse than an unbeliever" (1 Th. 5:8 TEV).

3. *On service*

"And let us not grow weary in welldoing, for in due season we shall reap, if we do not lose heart. So then, as we have opportunity, let us do good to all men, and especially to those who are of the household of faith" (Gal. 6:9-10 RSV).

4. *On fellowship*

"And let us consider how to stir up one another to love and good works, not neglecting to meet together, as is the habit of some, but encouraging one another" (Heb. 10:24-25 RSV).

5. *On study*

"Yes, if you cry out for insight and raise your voice for understanding, if you seek it like silver and search for it as hidden treasures, then you will understand the fear of the Lord and find the knowledge of God" (Pr. 2:3-6 RSV).

6. *On finances*

"Give me neither poverty nor riches; feed me with the food that is needful for me, lest I be full and deny thee, and say 'Who is the Lord?' or lest I be poor and steal and profane the name of my God" (Pr. 30:8-9 RSV).

7. *On health*

"Do you know that your body is a temple of the Holy Spirit within you, which you have from God? You are not your own; you were bought with a price. So glorify God in your body" (1 Cor. 6:19-20 RSV).

My Response:

STEP SEVEN
LEARN TO PRAY

"He was praying
in a certain place, and
when he ceased, one of
his disciples said to him,
Lord, teach us to pray...."
Luke 11:1 (RSV)

STEP SEVEN: LEARN TO PRAY

Suppose you met a man who said he was deeply in love with a wonderful girl, and he described their relationship this way: "I really don't enjoy talking to her all that much. In fact when I do I often fall asleep. Sometimes I don't see her for several days. When I do, I ask her for a lot of things, but I don't listen to her. When I do listen my mind wanders a lot. She writes beautiful letters, but I don't get around to reading them often. I take her to a big party every Sunday, but I don't have much time to be alone with her. But I sure love her."

You would certainly question the quality of his love. If you want love to work you have to spend time on it. If loving God has become the ideal of your whole life, then your whole life is concerned with building a loving relationship with God. If this is so, then prayer is the most important thing you do every day.

Prayer is spending time with God. Most people have difficulty with prayer because they leave it to chance. Probably the single most important decision you can make if you want to grow in your Christian life is to commit yourself to a daily time of personal prayer.

A regular time of prayer is not just something for the clergy or especially holy people. Prayer is part of a normal Christian life. It is not just for extra credit or emergencies. It is the cornerstone of a committed Christian life.

Many, perhaps most, Christians never learn to pray. "Everything I do is a prayer." "I can only use formal written prayers." "I'm too busy." "I tried but nothing happened."

There are usually one or more problems at the root of those attitudes: a basic weakness in faith, unrepented sin, a disorganized life, lack of a good prayer method or lack of perseverance.

The solutions to these root problems are to exercise more faith, repent of sin if necessary, put order in your life, find a good prayer method, and persevere.

If you want to learn to pray, then the first step is to make a decision to pray every day. Choose the time of day that works best for you, a time when you are able to stay alert. Give God at least 30 minutes of your prime time. Ask others to protect you from phone calls and visitors.

Next, choose a place. Find a place that is quiet, a place where you can be free from interruptions and distractions. For years my family has had a prayer room. Sometimes it has been a large closet, sometimes a corner of the basement that has been walled off.

Next, choose a method that will be helpful. There are a lot of misconceptions about prayer today. Many of them originate in Eastern thought or in popular psychology. Prayer is not thinking nice thoughts about God, feeling warm and gooey, doing mental or emotional calisthenics or engaging in self-development.

Rather, prayer is investing yourself wholly and entirely and sincerely in getting in touch with God. The traditional definition is a good one: "the lifting up of the mind and heart to God." By the power of God's Spirit, we do this in the five major forms of prayer: praise, repentance, thanksgiving, listening and petition.

God provides you with both the grace to pray and with a sense of his presence, giving you his peace, consolation, direction and forgiveness.

There are many good prayer methods. Some of them are quite ancient. One of the earliest, the *lectio continua*, involves prayerfully reading Scripture until something strikes you and then meditating on that passage before continuing. Another method is to repeat a prayer, such as the Our Father, very slowly and to meditate on each word or phrase. There is also repetitive prayer, such as the Jesus Prayer, which helps us to focus on a deeper theme while repeating the words of the prayer.

Here is one of the most helpful prayer methods I have found. It takes from 20 to 30 minutes to use it, and involves the five forms of prayer in sixteen steps, each of which requires a minute or two.

First, dress comfortably and choose a position that helps you: standing, kneeling or sitting. Change your position as often as it is helpful to do so.

STEP SEVEN: LEARN TO PRAY

1) Remember that you are in God's presence with all his saints and angels glorifying him. Remember that there are millions of men, women and children around the world who are in prayer at the same time you are turning to the Lord.

2) Thank God for bringing you to this moment and for all the good he has done to you all the days of your life.

3) Briefly consider your faults. Resolve to be reconciled with others.

4) Ask the Holy Spirit to fall upon you.

5) Praise God.

6) Ask God if there is anything he wants to talk to you about today.

7) Sing a spiritual song.

8) Call to mind the good things God has been doing for you and others.

9) Thank God for all he is doing.

10) Listen to the Lord. Ask him to speak to you.

11) Turn to a passage in Scripture.

12) Thank God for what he has revealed to you.

13) Pray for the needs of others and for your needs.

14) Thank God for having heard your prayer.

15) Turn to another passage in Scripture or ask the Lord to call one to your mind. Ask the Lord to speak clearly to you, in case you have somehow missed what he wanted to say to you.

16) Conclude with the Lord's Prayer.

Prayer is a work of the Holy Spirit who "helps us in our weakness; for we do not know how to pray as we ought" (Rm. 8:26 RSV). It is the simplicity of talking and listening to God as a person.

Ten long boring conversations with someone won't make a friendship, but if you are honestly open with someone in revealing who you are and if you really listen to that person, real friendship can result.

Christian prayer is a conversation with another person, Jesus. It dies if it becomes merely introspection. Many people find prayer boring because it is self-centered. (Have you ever talked to someone who is not listening?) Prayer is meant to be a

STEP SEVEN: LEARN TO PRAY

dialogue in which you honestly and spontaneously share, listen and respond.

Don't become enslaved by a prayer method. Be open to the surprising work of the Spirit and feel free to respond. God may want to take your conversation in a different direction.

Prayer: Lord, I want to learn to pray. I want to be faithful to a daily time of prayer. Help me to choose a time and place and method that will bring me closer to you. Send your Spirit to help me, and strengthen me to persevere.

DAILY MEDITATION

1. *Will God help me to learn to pray?*

"Likewise the Spirit helps us in our weakness; for we do not know how to pray as we ought" (Rm. 8:26 RSV).

2. *When should I pray?*

"Pray constantly, give thanks in all circumstances; for this is the will of God in Christ Jesus for you" (1 Th. 5:17-18 RSV).

3. *How should I pray?*

Praise: "Praise the Lord! O servants of the Lord, praise the name of the Lord for this time forth and forevermore! From the rising of the sun to its setting the name of the Lord is to be praised" (Ps. 113:1-4 RSV).

4. *How should I pray?*

Repent: "Have mercy on me, O God, according to thy steadfast love; according to thy abundant mercy blot out my transgressions. Wash me thoroughly from my iniquity and cleanse me from my sins!" (Ps. 51:1-2 RSV).

5. *How should I pray?*

Thank: "O give thanks to the Lord, for he is good; for his steadfast love endures forever!" (Ps. 106: 1 RSV).

6. *How should I pray?*

Listen: "Be still before the Lord, and wait patiently for him" (Ps. 37:7 RSV).

7. *How should I pray?*

Ask: "Have no anxiety about anything, but in everything by prayer and supplication with thanksgiving let your requests be made known to God. And the peace of God, which passes all understanding, will keep your hearts and minds in Christ Jesus" (Ph. 4:6-7 RSV).

My Response:

WALKING ON

"But the path of the righteous is like the light of dawn which shines brighter and brighter until full day."
Proverbs 4:18 (RSV)

A Christian marriage counselor said that he believed there were five stages in marriage: illusion, disillusion, waiting, acceptance and agape. He said that very often two people marry their images of each other and that typically within one year the second stage, disillusion, sets in as they begin to see flaws in each other.

The third stage, waiting, can go on for years. Each partner in the marriage waits for the other to change because, if he or she does, we can work things out. The fourth stage occurs when the partners accept each other as they are and decide to honor their covenant. If this occurs the fifth stage, agape, is possible—two people loving each other selflessly. He said that giving 50/50 was a truce, but 100/100 a marriage.

Your relationship with God can be like that. You meet Jesus as brother, friend, savior and all is well until you begin to see the "fine print" and realize what his Lordship means. You can try to "outwait" God, or hope that his conditions will change. They won't. God wants a 100/100 covenant with you. You simply need to accept that fact.

In baptism God has called you to love him with your whole mind, heart and strength. When you accepted his salvation he commanded you to be reconciled to him and to put on his mind. You are called to holiness.

When a young man I know was attending college, a leader in campus ministry quoted these words to him, "There is only one sorrow—the sorrow of not being a saint." Before he graduated that young man said to me, "I'd like to do something great for Christ with my life." I hope something like that has happened in your heart.

In our day there are a great many spiritual movements, causes and organizations. Christians are doing lots of spiritual things. What God wants in the church today, however, are deeply spiritual men and women. It has always taken holy people to renew the church and we won't get by with less today.

If you want to answer the Lord's call to holiness of life, if you want to make loving

God the ideal of your life, then you need to begin to give God the best yes you can in all the circumstances of your life.

An old preacher said, "God is always voting for you. The devil is always voting against you. How you vote decides the contest."

You can decide to give God your best "yes" and still ask the question, "How can I with all my weaknesses ever love God the way he should be loved?"

You need to remember that you *grow* in your relationship with God. It is a lifetime process. God is patient with you. He is not nervous and he is not deaf. He wants you to be patient with yourself and with everyone you encounter.

You can't grow in holiness through your own efforts alone. They are required, but your progress in loving God depends primarily on your openness to and cooperation with the working of God's Holy Spirit living in you. If you attempt this on your own strength, you will become impatient, frustrated and discouraged.

You must believe that the Holy Spirit is

living in you and is actively transforming you. To grow in loving God you must learn to rely daily on the power of the Holy Spirit. For God "is able to do so much more than we can ever ask for, or even think of, by means of the power working in us" (Eph. 3:20 RSV).

May you know the love of Christ which surpasses knowledge, and may you be filled with the fullness of God.